A MAN CAN BE...

by Susan Kempler   Doreen Rappaport   Michele Spirn

photographs by Russell Dian

HUMAN SCIENCES PRESS
72 FIFTH AVENUE,
NEW YORK, N.Y. 10011

Kempler, Susan.
    A man can be....

    SUMMARY: Text and photographs illustrate the
emotions and characteristics of a man.
    1. Men—Psychology—Juvenile literature.
[1. Emotions. 2. Men] I. Rappaport, Doreen, joint
author. II. Spirn, Michele, joint author. III. Dian,
Russell. IV. Title.
BF692.5.K45   155.3′32   80-25356
ISBN 0-89885-046-0

To Steve and Josh

and to Ari, Ilan and Daniel and the memory of their father, John.

The Authors wish to thank Bob and Geoffrey Eakin and Rick and Pharoah Cranston for their help.

A man can be lazy

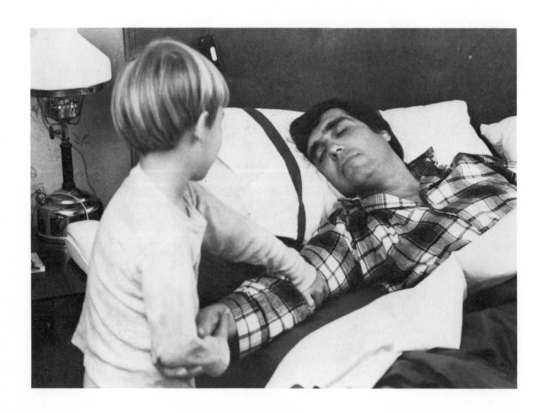

and loving

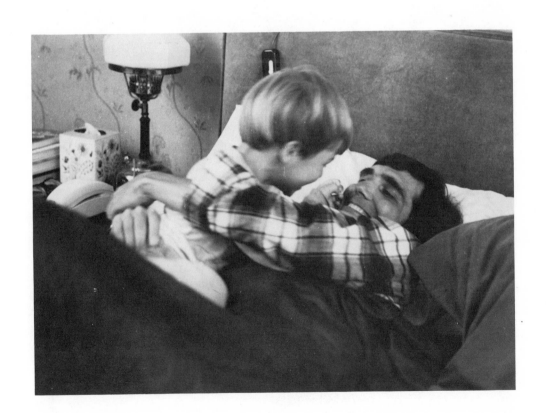

and silly

and serious.

He can be handy

and clumsy

and neat.

A man can be angry
and scold you

and then forgive you.

He can be helpful

and not so helpful.

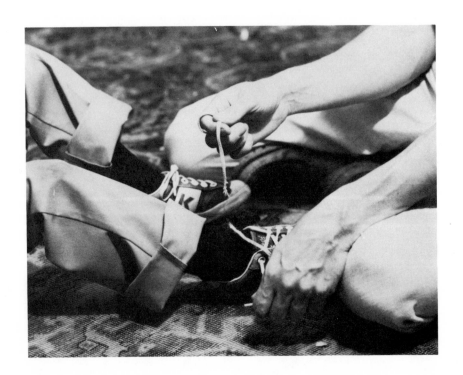

A man can be friendly
and affectionate.

He can be

playful

and daring

and careful.

A man can understand crying,

feel sad when you hurt
and be gentle.

He can share listening

and talking.

He can be quiet

and moody

and want to be alone.

He can feel close

and be tender.

A man is

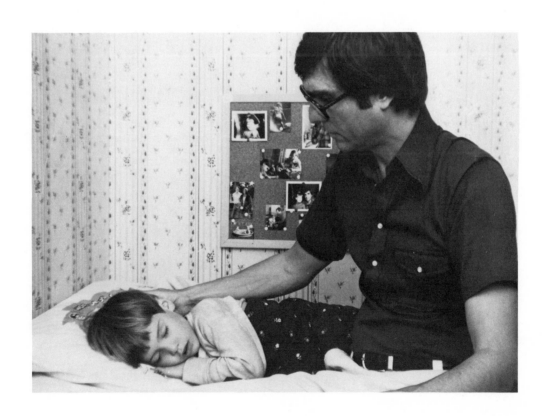

what a boy will be

someday.

▦ Human Sciences Press Children's Books

Arnstein, Helene

BILLY AND OUR NEW BABY
Illustrated by M. Jane Smyth
0-87705-093-7 $9.95   1973
Ages 4 to 8

Barrett, John M.

DANIEL DISCOVERS DANIEL
Pictures by Joe Servello
0-87705-423-1 $9.95   1979
Ages 5 to 10

NO TIME FOR ME
Illustrated by Joe Servello
0-87705-385-5 $9.95   1979
Ages 4 to 8

OSCAR THE SELFISH OCTOPUS
Pictures by Joseph Servello
0-87705-335-9 $9.95   1978
Ages 4 to 8

Beaudry, Jo, and Lynne Ketchum

CASEY GOES TO COURT
Illustrated with photographs by Jack Hamilton
0-89885-088-6 $9.95   1982/June

Berger, Terry

I HAVE FEELINGS
Illustrated with photographs by I. Howard Spivak
0-87705-021-X $9.95   1971
Ages 4 to 8

I HAVE FEELINGS TOO
Illustrated with photographs by Michael Ach
0-87705-441-X $9.95   1979
Ages 4 to 8

Bergstrom, Corinne

LOSING YOUR BEST FRIEND
Illustrated by Patricia Rosamilia
0-87705-471-1 $9.95   1980
Ages 4 to 8

Berman, Linda

THE GOODBYE PAINTING
Illustrated by Mark Hannon
0-89885-074-6 $9.95   1982/June

Blue, Rose

ME AND EINSTEIN
Illustrated by Peggy Luks
0-87705-388-X $9.95   1979
Ages 8 and up

WISHFUL LYING
Illustrated by Laura Hartman
0-87705-473-8 $9.95   1980
Ages 4 to 8

Boyd, Selma and Pauline Boyd

THE HOW
Making the Best of a Mistake
Illustrated by Peggy Luks
0-87705-176-3 $9.95   1981/April
Ages 4 to 8

Fassler, Joan, Ph.D.

ALL ALONE WITH DADDY
Illustrated by Dorothy Lake Gregory
Revised Edition
0-87705-009-0 $9.95   1971
Ages 4 to 8

BOY WITH A PROBLEM
Illustrated by Stewart Kranz
0-87705-054-6 $9.95   1971
Ages 4 to 8

DON'T WORRY DEAR
Illustrated by Stewart Kranz
0-87705-055-4 $9.95   1969
Ages 4 to 8

THE MAN OF THE HOUSE
Illustrated by Peter Landa
Revised Edition
0-87705-010-4 $9.95   1969
Ages 4 to 8

MY GRANDPA DIED TODAY
Illustrated by Stewart Kranz
0-87705-053-8 $9.95   1971
Ages 4 to 8

ONE LITTLE GIRL
Illustrated by M. Jane Smyth
0-87705-008-2 $9.95   1969

Fink, Dale Borman

MR. SILVER AND MRS. GOLD
Illustrated by Shirley Chan
0-87705-447-9 $9.95   1980
Ages 4 to 8

Gatch, Jean

SCHOOL MAKES SENSE... SOMETIMES
Illustrated by Susan Turnbull
0-87705-494-0 $9.95   1980
Ages 4 to 10

Gold, Phyllis

PLEASE DON'T SAY HELLO
Illustrated with Photographs by Carl Baker
0-87705-211-5 $9.95   1975
Ages 6 to 10

Goldsmith, Howard

TOTO THE TIMID TURTLE
Illustrated by Shirley Chan
0-87705-524-4 $9.95   1981
Ages 4 to 8

Green, Phyllis

A NEW MOTHER FOR MARTHA
Illustrated by Peggy Luks
087705-330-8 $9.95   1978
Ages 4 to 8

Greenberg, Polly

I KNOW I'M MYSELF BECAUSE...
Illustrated by Jennifer Barrett
0-89885-045-2 $9.95   1981/July
Ages 2 to 6

Greene, Laura

CHANGE
Getting to Know about Ebb and Flow
Illustrated by Gretchen Mayo
087705-401-0 $9.95   1981/April
Ages 4 to 8

HELP
Getting to Know about Needing and Giving
Illustrated by Gretchen Mayo
087705-402-9 $9.95   1981/April
Ages 4 to 8

Hazen, Barbara Shook

IT'S A SHAME ABOUT THE RAIN
Illustrated by Bernadette Simmons
0-89885-050-9 $9.95   1982/January

IF IT WEREN'T FOR BENJAMIN
(I'd Always Get to Lick the Icing Spoon)
Illustrated by Laura Hartman
0-87705-384-7 $9.95   1977
Ages 4 to 8

TWO HOMES TO LIVE IN
A Child's-Eye View of Divorce
Illustrated by Peggy Luks
087705-313-8 $9.95   1977
Ages 4 to 8

VERY SHY
Illustrated by Sue Rotella
0-89885-067-3 $9.95   1982/January

Horner, Althea J.

LITTLE BIG GIRL
Illustrated by Patricia C. Rosamilia
0-89885-098-3 $9.95   1982/June

"I and the Others" Writer's Collective

IT'S SCARY SOMETIMES
Illustrated by the children themselves
0-87705-366-9 $9.95   1978
Ages 4 to 8

Jacobson, Jane

CITY, SING FOR ME
A Country Child Moves to the City
Illustrated by Amy Rowen
0-87705-358-8 $9.95   1978
Ages 6 to 10

Leggett, Linda and Linda Andrews

THE ROSE-COLORE[D] GLASSES
Melanie Adjusts to Poor Vision
Illustrated by Laura Hartman
087705-408-8 $9.95
Ages 8 and up

Levine, Edna S., Ph.D., Litt.D.

LISA AND HER SOUNDLESS WORL[D]
Illustrated by Gloria Kamen

A Children's Book of the Year, 197[?] Award Granted by the Childre[n] Book Committee of the Child Stu[dy] Association of America.

0-87705-104-6 $9.95

Menzel, Barbara

WOULD YOU RATHER?
Illustrated by Sumishta Brahm
0-89885-076-2 $9.95   1982/Jan[.]

Rappaport, Doreen, Susan Kempler an[d] Michele Spirn

A MAN CAN BE ...
Illustrated with photographs by Russell Dian
0-89885-046-0 $9.95   1981[?]
Ages 2-6

Rappaport, Doreen

BUT SHE'S STILL M[Y] GRANDMA
Illustrated by Bernadette Simmons
0-89885-072-X $9.95   1982/Jan[.]

Sheehan, Cilla, M.A.C.P.

THE COLORS THAT [I] AM
Illustrated by Glen Elliot
089885-047-0 $10.95   1981[?]
Ages 4 to 10

Soderstrom, Mary

MAYBE TOMORRO[W] I'LL HAVE A GOOD TIME
Illustrated by Charlotte Epstein Wein[?]
0-89885-012-6 $9.95   1981[?]

Stefanik, Alfred T.

COPYCAT SAM
Illustrated by Laura Huff
0-89885-058-4 $9.95   1982/Jan[.]

Strauss, Joyce

HOW DOES IT FEEL...
Illustrated by Sumishta Brahm
0-89885-048-7 $9.95   1981[.]
Ages 4 to 8

Wittels, Harriet and Joan Greisman

THINGS I HATE
Illustrated by Jerry McConnel
0-87705-096-1 $9.95
Ages 4 to 8

Complete Children's Catalog available upon request